T0095250

HAVING IT GOOD
DOWNRANGE

HAVING IT GOOD
DOWNRANGE

A ONE-YEAR MILITARY TOUR IN IRAQ

PAUL BOUCHARD

HAVING IT GOOD DOWNRANGE
A ONE-YEAR MILITARY TOUR IN IRAQ

Copyright © 2015 Paul Bouchard.

All rights reserved. No part of this book may be used or reproduced by any means, graphic, electronic, or mechanical, including photocopying, recording, taping or by any information storage retrieval system without the written permission of the publisher except in the case of brief quotations embodied in critical articles and reviews.

iUniverse books may be ordered through booksellers or by contacting:

iUniverse
1663 Liberty Drive
Bloomington, IN 47403
www.iuniverse.com
1-800-Authors (1-800-288-4677)

Because of the dynamic nature of the Internet, any web addresses or links contained in this book may have changed since publication and may no longer be valid. The views expressed in this work are solely those of the author and do not necessarily reflect the views of the publisher, and the publisher hereby disclaims any responsibility for them.

Any people depicted in stock imagery provided by Thinkstock are models, and such images are being used for illustrative purposes only. Certain stock imagery © Thinkstock.

ISBN: 978-1-4917-3400-1 (sc)
ISBN: 978-1-4917-3399-8 (e)

Library of Congress Control Number: 2014908601

Print information available on the last page.

iUniverse rev. date: 03/24/2015

For Tony, Steve, Bennett, Mike, and Amy.

Author's Note

In writing about my one-year military tour in Iraq, I have done my best to recollect events and recreate dialogue as I remember them. The views expressed in this article are my own and not those of the US Army.

We sleep safely at night because rough men stand ready to visit violence on those who would harm us.

Winston S. Churchill

It really hit me when we were watching the movie *Restrepo*.

The *it* I'm referring to is the realization of how good I had it during my one-year military deployment to Iraq from 2010 to 2011.

We were four JAG captains, two paralegals, and our regional defense counsel (RDC)––a lieutenant colonel–– sitting around a large-screen TV in the Trial Defense Service (TDS) Office in Camp Victory, Iraq. The seven of us were eating pizza and popcorn and watching *Restrepo*, a documentary based on Sebastian Junger's book *War*. The movie is a true account of the soldiers of Second Platoon, B Company, 503rd Infantry Regiment of the 173rd Airborne Brigade Combat Team, and their combat experiences in Afghanistan's Korangal Valley. The movie is named after one of the Second Platoon soldiers, PFC Restrepo, who died in combat in that dangerous, enemy-infested valley.

There I was, enjoying pizza and popcorn in a nice, comfortable, air-conditioned office, watching a movie featuring soldiers who were direct participants in combat. Theirs was a world of constant enemy fire and dangerous patrols, while I—stationed at a large American military camp outside of Baghdad—had so many comforts.

We had great mess halls at Camp Liberty and Camp Victory; they were equivalent to IHOP for breakfast and Golden Coral for lunch and dinner. Friday dinners were surf 'n' turf, and fast food from Taco Bell, Pizza Hut, Burger King, and Cinnabon was readily available. We also had Green Beans, a coffee house similar to Starbucks, Northend, a pizzeria run by Filipinos, and a cigar lounge that resembled the inside of a Sheraton Hotel. And across the street from the cigar lounge was a row––basically an entire block––of buildings featuring a souvenir shop, a men's clothing store run by Turks, an Iraqi restaurant popular for its pizza, and a Chinese food establishment. I bought two tailor-made suits at the men's clothing store.

We had five-kilometer races and softball leagues, and the migrant workers—Ugandan security guards, the Indians and Pakistanis who worked in the mess halls, and Filipinos and Filipinas who did our laundry—had soccer leagues. Our Morale, Welfare, and Recreation (MWR) offices had well-equipped gyms, table games like ping pong, popular board games, poker nights, and well-stocked mini libraries featuring tons of popular paperbacks. I played poker twice a week.

MWR and USO[1] also hosted entertainment events for us like professional BMX[2] bike riders displaying their long jumps and back flips, a comedy show with an introduction by Lance Armstrong and featuring Robin Williams with some other comedians, and a few concerts. I saw Smash Mouth (they were great), and Toby Keith (not only a talented singer and guitarist but funny too).

Our living quarters were comfortable; we lived in air-conditioned trailers called containerized housing units (CHUs). A CHU generally featured a bed, a small table, a desk, a television set, and Internet service, the latter costing around $20 a month. We JAG Corps criminal defense attorneys didn't have roommates so we each had an air-conditioned CHU room all to ourselves.

---

[1]   The United Service Organizations Inc. (USO Show) is a nonprofit organization providing programs, services, and live entertainment to United States troops.

[2]   BMX or bicycle motocross is a cycle sport performed on BMX bikes, either in competitive BMX racing or freestyle BMX.

My buddies and I had it good, but being in a combat zone had its dangers, namely the possibility of receiving rocket fire from the bad guys (this could happen at any time), and being kidnapped (a danger that existed at night).

We always had to carry a weapon which for JAG officers was a 9 mm handgun. Occasionally we received reports of American servicemen being offered rides at night from foreign-looking men who spoke accented English. These were the kidnappers. On one occasion an American soldier had to pull his weapon on them.

When I was at Bagram Air Base in Afghanistan in 2006, the demarcation between the American base and the surrounding territory was always clear—the two were separated by fences and wire, and you always knew when you were "outside the wire," in enemy territory. But Camp Liberty and Camp Victory, Iraq, weren't like that; there were roads and more roads, buildings and warehouses, and the outskirts of Baghdad were close by. Simply put, there was no clear separation between the American bases and enemy territory. Because of this, my buddies and I always made sure we had our eyes on the drivers of the many trucks traveling on the numerous roads, ensuring the vehicles were driven by American servicemen or contractors and not civilians who might want to kidnap us. Luckily and fortunately, there weren't any successful kidnappings during my military tour in Iraq. There were, however, attempted kidnappings. We had to keep our eyes open, and we almost always walked in pairs.

But unquestionably, the biggest threat we faced was the possibility of being hit with shrapnel from enemy rocket rounds. If I had to guess, I'd say we were rocketed ten to fifteen times during my one-year deployment.

When I first arrived at Camp Liberty I had a conversation with the captain I was replacing:

> "So, what's the force protection situation here?" I asked. "I heard Camp Liberty gets its fair share of rocket fire."
>
> "That's affirmative," he said. "I'd say we get rocketed about once a month."
>
> "Oh, okay."
>
> "Yeah, some time back a round landed in our CHU area, about two hundred feet from my CHU, which will be your CHU."
>
> "How serious was that rocket fire?" I asked.
>
> "Pretty serious. One soldier died."

Once I was running in a five-kilometer race and the all-too-familiar warning signal of "Incoming! Incoming!

Incoming!" was blasted over the strategically placed loud speakers. Immediately, all the runners got down on their stomachs or sought cover in nearby concrete bunkers. After about a minute or so the signal "All clear! All clear! All clear!" was given, and the race resumed.

Twice the warning signal was given when I was playing poker. We players crouched down below the poker table or got down on our stomachs until we heard the all-clear signal.

Two more rocket attacks stick out in my mind—one when I was jogging around Signal Hill and the other when I was with colleagues at Camp Victory.

Signal Hill was a steep hill directly behind the Camp Liberty TDS Office. It was a communication center with numerous antennas and what looked like a cell-phone tower atop its pinnacle. It was a favorite target of the bad guys and was sporadically subject to enemy rocket fire. It was also surrounded by a one-mile asphalt track shaped like a horseshoe, making it a popular site for jogging.

I often jogged around Signal Hill in the evening, enjoying the cooler nighttime temperatures and seeing the beautiful sunsets––Iraq did have gorgeous sunsets. Many soldiers jogged around Signal Hill, and army physical fitness tests (APFTs) were often given there because the necessary two-mile run could be orchestrated easily around Signal Hill. But all of us knew it was a sought-after rocket target, something that was frequently in the back of our minds.

One evening while I was jogging around Signal Hill the warning signal was blasted and in seconds I sought cover under a nearby palm tree. A soldier I didn't know, riding a bicycle for his evening workout, sought cover under the same tree.

Seconds passed and nothing happened. Bent down under the palm tree, we didn't talk––we were just waiting for the all-clear signal so we could resume our activities. Suddenly, from my ten o'clock position, I saw a ball of orange fire maybe a mile and a half away over flatlands and the man-made "Z Lake" named for its shape.[3] More seconds passed, and then came the loud siren sounds of a fire truck. The truck passed by us at a brisk speed, heading down to the site of the rocket-caused fire.

From my vantage point I could see the flames were not spreading. I was also familiar with the site of the fire––a warehouse district, luckily not a residential CHU area. A few minutes passed and then the all-clear signal was given. I jogged straight to the TDS Office and called

---

[3] The beautiful small lake shaped like a Z was a welcome sight compared to the barren dry lands surrounding Camp Liberty and Camp Victory. Saddam Hussein and his sons supposedly used to water ski on the lake.

my TDS counterparts, informing them I was okay.[4] The incident marked the first and only time I saw the end result of a rocket attack.

The other rocket attack of note occurred one morning when I was working at the Camp Victory TDS Office. Three attorneys (I was one of them), one paralegal, and two soldier clients were in the building. All of a sudden the "Incoming! Incoming! Incoming!" signal came over the loudspeakers, and all of us immediately stopped what we were doing and headed downstairs to the basement. Reacting to rocket fire is similar to taking precautions against an incoming tornado: seek cover—basements are safer than higher levels—and stay away from windows that can shatter.

We were in the basement, crouched down, waiting for the all clear signal. It was silent; no one talks during a rocket attack. Then, out of nowhere, an unmistakable whistling sound buzzed over our building.

Previously, some soldiers told me they had actually heard rocket rounds during earlier attacks, but I'd never experienced that. I had seen a fire caused by a rocket attack, but I had never actually heard the sounds of rocket

---

[4]   Such notification was necessary because after a rocket attack we had to report to the higher chain of command that all personnel were accounted for.

rounds. But now, crouched down in the basement of the Camp Victory TDS Office, I heard the incoming round. One couldn't miss it––it was a fast whistling sound that lasted a few seconds.

I thought about what Erich Maria Remarque wrote in *All Quiet on the Western Front*: there's nothing scarier than facing artillery fire. This wasn't artillery fire, and I actually felt safe. But I didn't want to hear whistling sounds again; I wanted to hear "all clear."

Later that day we found out the round(s) had landed across Z Lake and overshot the building housing our four-star general, about a third of a mile from where we were.

We were well defended in Iraq. I have to give a big shout out and thumbs up to Northrup Grumman, Raytheon, and the other defense contractors who kept us safe. And I send a huge thank you to whichever company developed the all-important counter rocket, artillery, and mortar (C-RAM) technology, because it definitely saved our butts many times.

I saw test runs of the C-RAM technology a couple of times––they were amazing; basically a string of rounds fired up in the sky, visible in the night hours because of tracers. C-RAM rounds were designed to shoot down incoming rounds. Amazing stuff. It helped keep us safe as did another piece of technology––a big white aerostat, smaller than the Goodyear Blimp, but big nevertheless. The aerostat was often up in the air, not too far from the environs of Signal Hill, keeping an eye on possible enemy activity.

❖

My buddies and I used two coping mechanisms to deal with our combat tours: lying and humor. Both were effective.

We had to lie to our families and friends back home. Who wants to hear, "Yes, Mom, it is dangerous here. Last night we were on the receiving end of a rocket attack, and there are kidnapping attempts too." Our loved ones back home worried enough about us as it was. Why make a tough situation worse?

One time a JAG buddy of mine was in his office at Camp Victory. It was after hours, and he was skyping with his girlfriend.[5] All of a sudden there was rocket fire, and the "Incoming!" warning signal was given. Did this JAG buddy of mine tell his girlfriend, "Honey, I gotta go.

---

[5] This JAG buddy of mine later married his then girlfriend. They had a beautiful wedding, complete with a military honor guard, of which I was a proud member.

We're getting rocketed"? Of course not. Instead he said something like, "Uh, honey, something came up. I gotta go. I'll call you back or Skype later."

We all lied because it made things easier for our loved ones back home.

<hr />

Humor was another tool we used to deal with our combat tours. I don't think it was planned or deliberate; it wasn't like, *Hey, I'm stressed out because I'm serving in combat, and I need a coping mechanism, so let me laugh and joke around just to deal with it.* Instead, joking around was something we did to keep things relaxed, to give our minds a break from the workload and the fact that we were in a combat zone.

During lunch breaks we'd joke around and tease one another. And on Friday nights we often ordered pizza and watched a movie as a group. The movies were usually comedies (*Restrepo* was an exception). We kept things relaxed. It was good.

The best example of humor came from our boss, the RDC, a very competent, popular, and well-liked lieutenant colonel.[6]

---

[6]   A year after our tour he was deservingly promoted to colonel.

RDC sent me an e-mail that said: "Paul, hot issue just came up. John, our defense counsel up in Mosul, just got physically threatened by one of his clients. Apparently his client has a propensity toward violence. I think he pointed his M-16 at John––something like that. I need you to go up there and help John out. It might get dangerous, but you're the right guy for this mission. Get on a bird up to Mosul ASAP, full battle rattle of course, and help John out. Good luck, and please acknowledge receipt of this e-mail. LTC F."

I read this e-mail quickly the first time, and then I read it again just to make sure I got it right. I thought, *Holy shit, one of our JAG defense counsels is being threatened by his own client.* My heart was racing. I stood at my desk and took a deep breath. I hit the reply button and typed:

"Sir, acknowledge receipt. I'm on it right away. Will get our paralegal to get me on a helo to fly out to Mosul ASAP. Caseload not too bad right now––I have second-chair defense counsels on all my cases. I'll pack quickly and be in Mosul as soon as possible. Respectfully, CPT Bouchard."

I hit the send button. My thoughts and movements were fast. I took my gear (K-pot and flak vest) off a nearby wood support stand. I also made sure my handgun holster had enough ammo pouches.

I walked quickly out of my office, headed down the short hallway to our paralegal, and told her to get me on a helicopter flight to Mosul immediately. I told her, "Pick the quickest one. If BIAP [Baghdad International Airport] has a quicker flight, then pick BIAP; if Camp Liberty has a sooner flight, then pick Liberty." I walked back to my office to wrap up some e-mails and start packing.

Suddenly my phone rang and I picked up the receiver. "Paul, it's me." It was our RDC. "Got you. You're too gullible. John's not in danger, there's no violent client." He was laughing. I was dumbfounded. "But see, Paul, that's why I like you. Loyal, man. No questions asked."

"Good one, sir," I mustered. "You got me." I smiled.

We did shit like that to keep things fun, and it made us worry less.

<hr/>

We were all subject to General Order Number 1, GO #1 for short, a written order that outlined the activities prohibited to us. The three most pertinent prohibitions––and the ones probably most frequently violated––were no sex, no alcohol, and no pornography.

One couldn't have sex while deployed unless one's spouse was also serving in the combat zone. I did know a JAG couple deployed together, so they could have sex without violating GO #1.

Actually, my understanding of the no sex prohibition was that one couldn't have sex "in his or her CHU." This naturally encouraged people to think about creative places to copulate. For instance, a JAG officer told me she once visited another TDS Office because of a case she was working on. As she entered the office she heard the unmistakable sounds of sexual intercourse coming from a nearby separate office room. She didn't make a scene, and she didn't open the door. She just waited in the hallway for the business at hand to end. Some fifteen minutes later two JAG officers stepped out of the office. An office is not a CHU so technically there was no GO #1 violation.

In my opinion the overwhelming majority of military service members complied with the rules, but some didn't. Sex did take place.

For example, the word on the street was that dance nights at the MWR facilities were popular places to hook up. Some of my soldier clients fed me the details:

> "The dance nights are popular, sir. Hip-hop night, salsa, country and western."
>
> "Sir, the uniform for dance nights is the PT [physical training] uniform, which, as you know, doesn't have rank. No fraternization violations, sir, because you don't know if you're dancing with an officer or an enlisted soldier."
>
> "Sir, you know the PT uniform–– black shorts, gray T-shirt, running shoes. Well at these dance nights some of the female soldiers pull up the back of their shorts, right up their butt cracks so we can see their asses. Makes them more attractive, you know. Those are the soldier-chicks who are looking to get some action."

One of my clients received administrative punishment for having sex with a Filipina migrant worker. Other soldier clients received similar punishments for similar violations. Depending on one's rank, administrative punishments like a written reprimand, extra duty, or a demotion could end one's military career.

Porn too was prohibited––couldn't possess it or watch it. We had Internet connectivity downrange, but service members knew the communications section had every right to monitor computer search terms on government computers. Whether the communications section also monitored service members' personal computers, I don't know. I do know I never had a soldier client charged with possessing porn. I attribute this to three things.

For one, the post exchanges and shoppettes carried magazines like *Maxim* and *Smooth,* the purchase and viewing of which did not violate GO #1. Second, the post offices definitely checked packages for any contraband including pornographic DVDs and magazines. I'm sure the post offices didn't intercept all contraband, but they did seem to have a high success rate.

One time a JAG buddy and I interviewed a soldier who worked at one of the post offices. We had teamed up as the defense counsels on a case, and this soldier was a witness. We interviewed him at the post office and I'll never forget how many porn DVDs were taped to the large plywood wall behind him.

"Contraband, I see," I told him.

He replied, "Yessir. We get a lot of those."

Third, a soldier told me how popular Skype was, and in the privacy of their CHUs—particularly when their roommates weren't around—guys basically could get sex shows from their wives or girlfriends back home.

Drugs were prohibited too, but some soldiers got clever, thinking that it was okay to consume spice[7] since it is not banned in the United States or mentioned in the Uniform Code of Military Justice (UCMJ) or GO #1. Midway through my tour in Iraq GO #1 was amended to include spice as a prohibited controlled substance, and the number of spice prosecutions noticeably dropped.

Consuming, importing, distributing, or manufacturing alcohol was also a GO #1 violation. One soldier took way too much fruit and sugar from the mess hall and attempted to set up a brewery in his CHU. He got into trouble for that. Some soldiers tried to get friends back home to mail alcohol to them, but as they did with marijuana or spice or porn DVDs, the post office staff had a keen eye for such violations. My understanding is they caught much of that

---

[7]   Spice is an herbal mixture that produces experiences similar to marijuana. It is also referred to as synthetic marijuana.

contraband too, and the soldiers who were the intended recipients of the contraband would face administrative or criminal punishments depending on the facts of the case.

There was another source of alcohol––Iraqi Christians and our allies, such as the British or Italians.[8] At times some of our soldiers, while out on patrol, would obtain alcohol from our allies or buy alcohol from families around Baghdad. (An Iraqi family with alcohol in the home had to be Christian, because Muslims do not consume or possess alcohol.)

One last note about alcohol––there were three occasions when the prohibition against it was not in effect: during a service member's two-week R&R vacation; if a service member was on pass status; and during the Super Bowl. I watched the Packers beat the Steelers with our RDC. The mess hall at Camp Victory had large-screen TVs set up for our Super Bowl viewing pleasure, and the two-beer maximum was strictly enforced.

<hr />

One Saturday night in the fall our entire office was invited to a social event hosted by the Carabinieri, the

---

[8] GO#1 didn't apply to our allies as we didn't have jurisdiction over them.

Italian police force stationed in Iraq to help the Iraqis establish a police force of their own. Our paralegal was sharp and popular, and she was friends with some of the Carabinieri, so through her we often got invited to such gatherings.

The Carabinieri-hosted outings were popular because they featured fresh handmade thin-crust pizzas made in an outdoor brick oven. Beer was available, as was nonalcoholic "near beer." (Nonalcoholic beer was not a GO #1 violation and was readily available in the mess halls). Water, juices, and sodas were also served, and cigar smoking was always popular at Carbinieri events.[9]

Our office——myself, our paralegal, and a talented army JAG officer named Steve——hopped in our assigned white Toyota pickup truck and headed to the Carbinieri's living quarters.

The place was quickly filling up when we got there. The Carabinieri, American service members, government employees, British contractors——the crowd was mixed, and the conversations were flowing. Our paralegal started mingling with her Italian acquaintances while Steve and

---

[9] There was a cigar club in Iraq, and social outings by the Carabinieri and the cigar club often coincided—same place, same time.

I got in line for the popular pizzas which were served hot right out of the oven.

Next to the oven were two large wooden picnic tables on which two of the Carabinieri were slicing the newly baked pizzas. There were coolers with drinks next to the tables. The line slowly inched forward, and Steve and I started talking about sports, politics, and stocks in which we might invest.

We both reached into a cooler for a drink. I forget what Steve was drinking, but I grabbed a dark green can, a nonalcoholic beer. I'd always liked pizza with beer, and "near beer" was the next best thing. Steve and I continued talking, sipping from our drinks, and inching up the line. Our paralegal was maybe thirty feet away, engaged in conversation with two Carabinieri members.

When we got to the picnic tables Steve and I grabbed paper plates and napkins, made our pizza selections––I chose two slices with tuna as the topping––and we sat at a nearby table. We started eating and we continued sipping from our drinks. The pizza was great as always.

A few minutes passed and then I told Steve, "You know, for nonalcoholic beer, this brew tastes pretty good." We continued talking and eating.

Suddenly I noticed our paralegal heading our way. Concern was written all over her face.

"Sir," she said, quietly so few could hear. "Do you know that's real beer you're drinking?" I immediately pulled the beer can close to my eyes so I could read it carefully. The brand was Carlsberg. I honestly thought it was a nonalcoholic beer, but I was reading the fine-print label to make sure. Steve started chuckling.

Damn, I thought. I read "Alcohol content of 5.5 percent." "Shit," I said out loud. My mind started racing:

> *Had anyone else seen me drinking? Man, I just violated GO #1. I thought for sure it was nonalcoholic; I knew it wasn't Heineken, because that's one of my favorites. Damn Italians. A GO #1 violation will bring me a written reprimand.*
>
> *I won't get promoted. My career will be finished. What will I do then? There is the defense of innocent ingestion. That's exactly what happened here. Good luck with that—no one will believe you innocently ingested alcohol especially since YOU'RE A FRIGGIN' JAG LAWYER! I'm screwed. Did anybody else see me drinking? Lots of senior officers here—they'll report the incident and my military career will be finished.*

I placed the beer can in a trash bin and got a bottle of water. Steve and our paralegal were chuckling. I knew they were thinking *This whole incident is funny; I hope things work out for you.* I was genuinely worried.

We stayed at the Italian social for maybe another hour, then we left. I worried all night. I tried to think about other things, but inevitably I'd always return to *Damn, I violated GO #1.*

I worried about the incident for a couple of days. In the end nothing came of it. I was grateful for that.

Saddam Hussein really was a bad guy, a tyrant.

The JAG lawyers assigned to the TDS offices in Iraq, Kuwait, and Afghanistan were getting together for a defense counsel conference at Camp Victory, Iraq. It was March 2011. We defense lawyers did some sightseeing around Camp Victory for a half day prior to the conference. We were part of a larger tour group that included contractors and civilian government employees.

Saddam had palaces all over Iraq but especially around Baghdad. That's basically the sightseeing we did, checking out some of Saddam's palaces. They were huge, opulent, and excessive.

Al-Faw Palace, named after Iraq's retaking of the Al-Faw Peninsula during the Iraq-Iran War in the 1980s, was close to Camp Victory's TDS Office. It had been converted to American military offices. Marble floors and columns stood out, and the palace had exceptional air conditioning. That was the first palace the group visited. My friends and I had visited it before, but not as part of a tour.

Immediately to the right as you entered the palace was a huge chair, a gold throne, with a comfortable felt-covered cushion. Sitting on the throne while getting your photo taken was a popular activity with visitors, but I wasn't into that. I felt it gave Saddam some legitimacy, something I didn't want to do.

I'd had the same reaction months earlier when my buddies and I visited Saddam's holding cell prior to his hanging.[10] His cell was spacious, but plain. He was allowed to walk into a small enclosed area with no roof so he could get some sun and fresh air. He was into plants, and he apparently watered flowers in pots in the enclosed area on a daily basis. Taking photos of his cell and of the flower plants was popular, but here too I was disinterested. I had read accounts of just how evil he and his two sons were, and I didn't care for mementos related to them.

---

[10]   Saddam Hussein was hanged in December of 2006.

Our group visited the palace interior for no more than an hour. To me the palace represented not only Saddam's egomania but also shoddy construction. A superior officer had informed me about this a couple of days earlier, and I agreed with his assessment.

From afar, Al-Faw Palace was striking, basically breathtaking. It gave one a *wow* feeling, because a viewer couldn't help but think, *Awesome. It's huge. It's beautiful. I wonder how long it took to build this palace.* Middle Eastern architecture can be striking with its tiled domes and tall steeples.

But when you entered the palace and looked at it with a critical eye, you had to notice the flaws and sloppy carpentry, especially where walls met ceilings and door frames. Large air gaps were evident, and caulking was nowhere to be found. Al-Faw Palace was like a so-so piece of art: impressive from afar but flawed upon close inspection.

Our group traveled in two vans, heading to another one of Saddam's many palaces. We stopped, got out of the van, and mingled into a sizeable crowd of military members, contractors, and civilian employees, all of us waiting for the tour guide. There were around thirty people. It was hot out, and nearly everyone carried a water bottle for necessary hydration. Minutes later the tour guide arrived. He was a young army soldier perhaps in his early twenties.

The tour guide led us into a large palace that was half in ruins, the result of effective American bombing earlier in the war. Chunks of concrete were piled up on both sides of our walking pathway. Here I took photos with my cheap disposal camera. High exposed ceilings were still intact, but I often looked upward, concerned that a chunk of debris might come crashing down.

The guide led us up a flight of wide concrete stairs. They were solid, but again I kept my eyes and ears alert for any signs of collapse. On the second floor we were lead outside to a large open deck where we could get a panoramic view of the environs––flat terrain and some palm trees below us, apartment complexes in Baghdad out in the distance, and three more impressive palaces to our right.

We walked around and many of us snapped photos. Then the guide said, "Right now, I'm pointing to the smaller palace, to the right, at my two o'clock position." We all looked at it. "That palace was used to house Saddam's prostitutes. Many young ladies used to live there."

We were led back inside and the guide showed us more rooms. Piles of crumbled concrete were never too far from our feet. Minutes later we were led to an adjacent building.

"Saddam hosted a lot of social events here," the guide told us. I noticed lots of pieces of broken glass next to our feet, the result of immense windows being shattered by bombs.

"Notice there is water all around us," the tour guide pointed out. "These are manmade canals surrounding this palace. Actually we are above water here, and there's a reason for that. In Islam, anything that happens on or above water is not seen and scrutinized by God. This building is above the canals, above water, so it is here that Saddam hosted his parties." The guide went on to inform us, "Young, beautiful girls were brought in to entertain Saddam's entourage. Booze, sex––nothing was off limits here, for God was not watching."

We were led down a wide hallway, with more piles of broken glass next to our feet. At one point during the tour the guide told us Saddam had always been alert and on the defensive, concerned he would be assassinated at any moment. "Security around him was always tight," said the guide. "Saddam was also afraid of germs, and he was often reclusive, rarely shaking hands with anyone, and not one to partake too often in the pleasures his parties offered." Apparently Saddam was a party host, but not that much of a partier.

The tour guide took us to a large room featuring a sizeable swimming pool lined with small square tiles, but the pool was empty of water. We positioned ourselves around the pool as the tour guide addressed us from a position close to the entrance.

A large indoor pool, I thought. *The comforts of being a rich tyrant. There were probably more parties here, pool parties.*

"This room was one of Saddam's many torture chambers," the young tour guide told us in a loud voice.

> Saddam would often meet with his high-ranking military officers in an adjacent room and discuss military plans. Saddam would purposefully say outrageous things––military plans that made no sense, military plans that would ensure defeat. Then the military officers were told to break into smaller groups and go into adjacent rooms to discuss military matters. What these military officers didn't know was Saddam and his henchmen had the rooms bugged, they were listening in, and any negative comments about Saddam and his military plans, any dissent, any criticism, anything like, "You know, Saddam our leader is wrong here; his plan will not work," anything like that and that military

officer was brought into this swimming-
pool room for some very difficult choices
and events.

The tour guide informed us the condemned military officer would be taken to the edge of the swimming pool with his hands and feet bound. His family, who probably lived in the Baghdad area, was taken there too.

"It didn't matter how long it took; his family was brought in, wife and kids," the guide told us. "Saddam did not tolerate dissent. Jacked-up military plans were a ploy. Saddam Hussein himself didn't necessarily believe in them; he just said outrageous things to test one's loyalty to him. Say anything bad about Saddam and you or your family paid a heavy price."

The military officer, his hands and feet still tied and bound, could see his family standing across from him on the other side of the empty pool. That's when the torture started––not on the officer, but on one of his family members. A son, a daughter, the wife––it didn't matter, because the events unfolded this way: a member of Saddam's trusted security team would grab the doomed family member's arm and steady it while another trusted security team member powered up the weapon of choice––an electric drill with a long drill bit. The driller would start at the victim's exposed elbow; the drill bit tore through skin and flesh and made its way through bone. Horrific screams and excruciating pain were the result, and the officer was forced to watch and listen to the horrors from the other end of the pool.

What followed next was the ultimatum: the torture of your family member can continue to no end, or you, disloyal military officer, can save your family by throwing yourself––headfirst––into the waterless pool.

"That explains why this pool was never filled with water," the guide told us. "Saddam was a swimmer, but this pool here was waterless and the site of many forced deaths."

The guide said he knew of no cases where the officer watched his entire family get tortured; each one eventually took the headfirst plunge to his death. "But often," the guide told us,

> it took more than one attempt, for some would fall awkwardly, the body's natural reaction to defend itself and avoid injury. Plunging head first into a ten-foot deep empty pool requires discipline. Many would fall but to their sides. That brought on more torture rounds to their family members, but the officer––assisted by guards––would be led back up to the

pool's edge for more head-first plunges until his neck fractured and death resulted. Quite often, even after hitting the pool's hard floor headfirst, the officer's body lay there, twitching, to the horror of his family members. The guards ensured that if the officer was unconscious but not dead, they'd pick up his twitching body, bring it back up to the pool's edge, and guide it to an accurate fall that would finally end the misery.

I didn't take photos of the torture-room swimming pool.

<hr />

It was a gruesome murder scene.

Two years before our combat tour a troubled American soldier had entered the Camp Liberty Combat Stress Office and killed five fellow soldiers. I'd heard the killer was unstable, and his unit chain of command had prudently removed his weapon from him, but, undeterred, he managed somehow to steal an M-16 rifle and kill five soldiers. Soldiers who seek counseling at Combat Stress Offices aren't allowed to carry weapons so the five victims were defenseless, sitting prey for the deranged killer.

Fast forward to two years later. The military criminal defense team visited Camp Liberty to investigate the crime scene. My buddies and I were there to help, driving team members around and assisting them with logistical needs.

The Combat Stress Office was some two hundred meters from our TDS Office, next to the chapel and the post office. My buddy and I drove the defense lawyer and the two civilians who were experts in bullet trajectories to the crime-scene building. The building had been locked and shut down immediately after the awful crime. A Criminal Investigative Division agent, already at the scene and waiting for us, unlocked the front door.

We entered. It was pitch-black inside, but someone flicked on a switch, and to my surprise the light bulbs–– unused for such a long time––still functioned. Thick, gray dust was everywhere. As I recall the government/ prosecution was contemplating charging the defendant, who was in pre-trial confinement, with the death penalty.

Before we knew it the two civilians were busy making measurements, taking notes, and connecting pieces of string from one bullet hole to another. I was amazed to see how fast they found bullet holes in the raw unpainted plywood walls.

My JAG buddy and I walked around the inside of the small building with the military defense lawyer. More light switches were turned on. There was no air conditioning and no air circulation. The place was dusty and stuffy.

Five soldiers were killed here, I kept thinking. *And by a fellow soldier.*

We turned a corner and entered a small room. A desk and chair occupied one corner. My eyes zeroed in on flakey black chips on the plywood floor next to the chair. The chips looked like the byproduct of dust, like dust balls glued together and pressed into flakes, only the flakes were darker than dust, not gray, but black, and not glossy; there was no sheen to them. They were in bunches, in thin, spread-out piles, forming a sort of line. There was definitely a pattern to them.

"What's that?" I asked the defense lawyer.

"That's the end result of dried-out blood," he responded. "That's what blood does if left alone on impenetrable surfaces; it dries out, turns black, and curds up."

There was an odd silence; then we left the building. I was glad to get out of there; the place had an eerie feeling to it.

<hr>

It was the first week of May 2011, and there was one week left of my Iraq tour. I was eating breakfast at the Camp Liberty mess hall, around eight in the morning.

Four or five flat-screen TVs hung on the walls. Usually the TVs showed a variety of channels—CNN, FOX, and ESPN. This particular morning all the flat screens were on CNN because there was breaking news: Osama bin Laden's hiding place had been overrun, and the head of al-Qaeda was no longer.

We got him.

Everyone was happy, and the successful termination of bin Laden was the talk of the morning, indeed the entire day. When I arrived at work at the Camp Victory TDS Office, my JAG buddies and I were all proud of the successful execution of the raid.

———◆◈◆———

My buddies drove me to BIAP. It was time to leave and head back to my home station, Fort Bliss, in El Paso, Texas. Steve had left in January, while one of our more seasoned defense lawyers and our talented paralegal extended their tours to Afghanistan because the mission in Iraq was winding down. Two JAG buddies remained in Iraq, but they were scheduled to redeploy[11] in a couple months.

---

[11]   The correct military term for returning to one's home base after a military deployment is to "redeploy." The term is confusing because it doesn't mean "to deploy again."

We said our good-byes; they're never easy. You're glad to leave of course, and you remember the good times you shared together. But you worry about the buddies you leave behind and hope they'll be okay. Oddly, the rocket attacks increased in both frequency and intensity as our military pullout was underway. The chief of TDS had actually predicted this, saying, "The bad guys will want to hit us as we leave."

My itinerary was as follows: helicopter flight to a base in Kuwait, a bus ride to Kuwait International Airport (KIA), a long flight to Fort Benning, Georgia, for outprocessing, and then a flight to Fort Bliss.

When I boarded my flight at KIA I was a bit tired, but not overly so. I decided to perk up by ordering a coffee once we had achieved our requisite flying altitude. My game plan was to write down my thoughts about the year just past. Fifteen minutes later, with a coffee and notepad firmly on my seat tray, I started writing:

Iraq——hot and dusty; temps reached 125F.

Lots of roads at Camp Liberty/Camp Victory; different than Afghanistan.

Great team; great people to work with.

Great mess halls.

Comfortable CHUs; A/C good.

Z Lake makes for a nice view; man-made lake.

Green Beans Coffee, Taco Bell, Cinnabon; Pizza Hut, Northend Pizza.

MWR buildings popular. Hip-hop night, salsa night. Lots of dancing. Poker twice a week.

Cigar lounge was fun.

Smoked from a hookah––watermelon flavor the night I tried it out.

Got two nice tailored suits from a Turkish tailor.

Saw the BMX bike show twice; spoke to Lance Armstrong for maybe ten seconds; stood next to Robin Williams for a group photo.

We got rocketed on occasion; threat of kidnapping present; heard a round over us; saw a fireball, the result of rocketing.

We were well defended; big thanks for the C-RAMs. Never rode in an MRAP (mine-resistant ambush protected) vehicle, but they were effective. Word is Defense Secretary Gates made that call; he was right.

Vice President Biden visited a few times; didn't get to see him.

TDS conference went well; my buddy Bennett deserves all the credit.

Saw two concerts, Smash Mouth and Toby Keith; good times, great shows.

Saw some DVD movies with the team. *Restrepo* was the best; read the book too— well done by Sebastian Junger. Those guys had it tough; we had it good compared to them.

Migrant workers, Indians and Pakistanis, work the mess halls. Ugandans are security guards. Filipinas do the laundry. All Indians, Pakistanis, and Ugandans are men. The lines at the Western Union at the PX are long because the migrant workers send a lot of their wages back home to support their families.

Heard translators start at $168,000 per year; wish I spoke Arabic.

November to February basically winter which is the wet season; lots of mud because of the rains; foot brushes installed next to building entrances to brush mud off our boots.

Asked the Iraqi lady who cleaned our office whether she was Shia or Sunni, and she said firmly, "I am Christian! Saddam bad. USA good."

Church right next to TDS Office. I went to Mass almost every Sunday. Funny how that works——in a combat zone you get closer to the Almighty.

5k races popular. Italian social nights popular too. Me and my friggin' GO #1 violation; thank God I didn't get caught. Nice to have the eleventh commandment kick in; I truly appreciate the innocent ingestion defense.

Lots of work; we stayed busy.

Controversy over end-of-tour awards; no more Bronze Stars given after Sept. 2010 because combat operations officially over even if rocket attacks increased. Some JAGs were pissed they got ARCOMS (Army Commendation Awards), because they'd thought they were getting Bronze Stars.

Those were my notes, my entries. I sipped some coffee and reflected on the previous 365 days during the flight back home. At times I looked down at the notes I had written. It was a good year. No one got hurt; we all came back home safely. And being an army criminal defense attorney was very rewarding work.

As to the big picture policy question, who knows how things will turn out in Iraq? What I do know is this: the world is better off without Saddam Hussein and, on a more personal note, my buddies and I had it good downrange, and for that I'm very grateful.

Paul Bouchard is an army JAG lawyer and author of *Enlistment, Lessons Learned, A Package at Gitmo, The Boy Who Wanted to Be a Man*, and *A Catholic Marries a Hindu*. He and his wife live in Northern Virginia. Visit Paul Bouchard at **www.paulbouchard.com**.

Printed in the United States
By Bookmasters